THE MUSIC
OF HER RIVERS

Mary Burritt
Christiansen
Poetry Series

MARY BURRITT CHRISTIANSEN

POETRY SERIES | *Hilda Raz, Series Editor*

The Mary Burritt Christiansen Poetry Series publishes two to four
books a year that engage and give voice to the realities of living, working,
and experiencing the West and the Border as places and as metaphors.
The purpose of the series is to expand access to, and the audience for,
quality poetry, both single volumes and anthologies, that can be used
for general reading as well as in classrooms.

Also available in the Mary Burritt Christiansen Poetry Series:

to cleave: Poems by Barbara Rockman
After Party: Poems by Noah Blaustein
The News As Usual: Poems by Jon Kelly Yenser
Gather the Night: Poems by Katherine DiBella Seluja
The Handyman's Guide to End Times: Poems by Juan J. Morales
Rain Scald: Poems by Tacey M. Atsitty
A Song of Dismantling: Poems by Fernando Pérez
Critical Assembly: Poems of the Manhattan Project by John Canaday
Ground, Wind, This Body: Poems by Tina Carlson
MEAN/TIME: Poems by Grace Bauer

For additional titles in the Mary Burritt Christiansen Poetry Series,
please visit unmpress.com.

Renny Golden

THE MUSIC

OF HER RIVERS

poems

*For Randy —
In gratitude for
your many years
of commitment
to social justice
¡Adelante!
Renny*

University of New Mexico Press   Albuquerque

Library of Congress Cataloging-in-Publication Data

Names: Golden, Renny, author.
Title: The music of her rivers: poems / Renny Golden.
DESCRIPTION: Albuquerque: University of New Mexico
    Press, 2019. | Series: Mary Burritt Christiansen
    poetry series
IDENTIFIERS: LCCN 2019009214 (print) |
    LCCN 2019009617 (e-book) | ISBN 9780826360786
    (e-book) | ISBN 9780826360779 (pbk.: alk. paper)
CLASSIFICATION: LCC PS3557.O35935 (e-book) |
    LCC PS3557.O35935 A6 2019 (print) | DDC 811/.6—dc23
LC record available at https://lccn.loc.gov/2019009214

COVER ILLUSTRATION: *The Sound of the Rio Grande.*
    © Meinrad Craighead, all rights reserved.
    Photograph supplied courtesy
    Pomegranate Communications, Inc.
DESIGNED BY Mindy Basinger Hill
COMPOSED IN Adobe Caslon Pro

I do not know much about gods; but I think that the river
Is a strong brown god—sullen, untamed and intractable
T. S. ELIOT, *Four Quartets*

Consider rivers. They are always en route to
their own nothingness.
From the first moment
They are going home.
EAVAN BOLAND, *In a Time of Violence*

You have to become everything, you know, and the creatures
. . . So, you have to become that river, too.
ARUNDHATI ROY on *Democracy Now!*

CONTENTS

RIO GRANDE

*There was never a more holy age than our own
and never a less (holy).*
ANNIE DILLARD

When I knew Wolf* he was a boy whose
thick hair was the color of a night river.
Now on the brink of Cochiti manhood,
I watch his gangly silhouette among
the dancers who burst from the kiva
into a blaze of sun; on each knee
tortoise shells rattle with each step.
The boys' kirtles are white as gardenias,
their hair tangled with eagle feathers,
at each boy's throat, a shell of Bull's Eye Malachite.

On cue they raise arms tied with pine branches,
keeping time to drums' pounding beat.
They move in a circle fluid as water,
self-forgetful boys becoming one voice chanting.
Wolf does not know what the words mean.
He knows the ancestors are close, knows the dance
carries him beyond what he can express,
knows its exhilarating rubric will end
when sun turns the plaza magenta.

The translation of words is in their bodies
as they move in the language of rivers.

I once knew the exuberance of youth who keep ritual,
whose bodies speak what words cannot.
I was nineteen; we sang psalms in Latin.
Three hundred of us beneath stained-glass windows
that floated rainbow colors on the white scapulars
of our Dominican habits. Matins, Lauds, Vespers—

we never knew we were singing the songs of prophets,
of lovers, of a God who accompanied the wretched.
We knew only to sing in perfect A-flat.
We knew Gregorian chant inflections.
We kissed the floor if we disturbed the chant.
We ate our dinner on the floor if we dropped kneelers.
We kept the great silence, kept custody of the eyes.
Confessed our faults on our knees.
We did not know the meaning of the words we sang.

We understood ourselves as belonging to ancient promises.
We offered praise. We offered ourselves.

Wolf is the name of my Cochiti friend's nephew.

The monastery sits high above the Chama River.
We came for Easter Mass. Wisps of incense
floated over the Benedictines like breath.
The river passing below carried
its own account of emptying, of rising.

Does the river keep their loneliness,
their voices in pearled morning?

The abbott sang the gospel in Latin.
His sermon could not locate
the ordinary resurrections
we carry and that carry us.

Like the monks, the Chama has kept
its vow of stability: 110 million years
tumbling from the San Juan Mountains, a run past
Chama Canyon's shale, basalt, sandstone.
On the ridge, ponderosa pine, fir, mahogany,
Gambel oak—attentive acolytes. The Canyon's parishioners—
elk, cougars, badgers, bobcats, falcons, raccoons.

The Chama's liturgy is wordless. Is that where
to begin the story of resurrection, in this world's glory?

How to say it, the way we have lifted each other,
how we have died to hope, risen again and again.
The Chama turns southeast past Abiquiu,
past monastery bells, the exaltation of hermits;
passes with its radiant retinue—
brown trout, cooper hawks, kiskadees,
and orioles flashing black and gold.

The angel of history holds the Rio Grande's passenger list—
first peoples of Mets'ichi Chena, people of corn who drum

until twilight plunges violet where dancers in ceremonial dress
lay pine boughs, baldrics of rabbit fur, gourd rattles on the river.

Two shipwrecked men—Cabeza de Vaca and the Moor, Esteban—
walk through swamp scum, mud, hissing sand, across blades

of rock leaving footprints of blood. Starving skeletons—one dark as night,
the other pale as sand. The peoples of the Río de las Palmas feed them,

wash them like babies. In return the Spaniards become healers,
discovering in themselves a surprising compassion.

Who they saved, saved them.

MEINRAD'S CALL

for Meinrad Craighead

At night you heard *the river, the river.*
Twenty years a Benedictine
when the Rio Grande called.
A call to stillness and ceaseless farewells.

A hermit again where owl, wolf, and grey-eyed dogs
became your companions; where you painted
wild presence as if it were God's body,
Crow Mother, Our Lady of Guadalupe guarding thresholds

between the worlds. God's protectors are
fierce coyotes, phlegmatic elk, and jackrabbit acolytes
vigilant for listeners to her heartbeats.
Is it a dream, is it simply the vision of a mystic—

at times terrible, the rabbit devoured, at times
an incandescent river emptying to capaciousness.

1598

P'Osoge we called the river until pale men
wearing coats of knives came.
Their red-sashed horses pranced into the river;
great mastiffs, then bishops, a procession of crosses,

banners, armor, arabesques, canons—
a retinue of monkeys squealing, all creaking toward
the City of Gold. Later, Juan de Oñate
ordered us to yield our stored food,

which we refused, circled Oñate's soldiers, quiet
as wolves, then struck. Suffered a wolf's fate—
one foot of every Acoma man chopped off, women enslaved.
We great grandsons of one-footed Pueblos dreamed

of trapped wolves, of sacred mountains' secret doors,
of the old ways, of eagle feathers, masks, of counting the days
until 1680—then Pueblo stampede, thunderous as wild horses,
wheeling beyond rifle shot, circling back,

smashing Spanish soldiers, priests, governors
with the surprise of our united fury,
the strategic brilliance
of the weak.

The river took the blood, cleansed the bodies.

I see ancient dancers come from aspen groves
mark time with their feet's tiny bells.
It is the holy season when they dress
with the river's gifts—turtle shells, feathers.

Soon I, too, will paint my chest sky blue,
yarrow yellow, pine green. Hours of chant
while our Cochiti drummers call eagle, fox, parrot spirits.
In spring I go with the men into cornfields that lie

below ochre-red buttes to dig out acequias until the river
rushes a flood of star-flecked waters into ditches.
I speak for this river carrying the stillborn, the dying—
this water that quenches the thirst of bosque, mergansers,

warblers, and ash-throated flycatchers.
What if the Sacred is a river cluttered
with rusted batteries, tires, paint cans,
bones of horses, oil, solvent, plastic bottles?

She rides on, cagey in her silence,
faithful as the wolf and as betrayed.
Here on the Otowi bridge, I watch
the river slip into darkness, its skin of stars.

You walk along the reedy paths of the Rio Grande,
Wolf, and watch ghosts come, the ones Bartolomé de las Casas
said are *guileless, the most devoid of hatreds.*
Your Navajo and Cochiti family argues all the time
about money or too many sleeping on the floor,
but they know what was done to their people.
I saw Spaniards cut off the nose and ears of Indians
without provocation.
This river is where it began.

John Muir said rivers flow, not past, but through us.
Let it flow through you
until it speaks:
I am as sacred as you expect,
as dangerous as they fail to imagine.
I am a receptacle of desires,
of detritus, precious lost things,
a ten-year-old boy who went under.
I can take you down, water your fields.
I am fearless as you need me less
for my body than my soul,
even as I choke toward the Gulf.

GOD'S MAP: A SONNET CROWN

River begins in snowmelt, washes over stone,
pours into San Juan cisterns, tarns, and moraines.
Drops, like falling hammers into gorge roar, a locomotive

of white water that slows, slows into sunlit silence,
pulls its traveling circus of muskrat, beaver, ducklings
across baked mud, mesquite, and tumbleweed;
loops and loops through it wild as God.

Wild as God, the river circles an ancient path
ever changing, slithers into dark basalt canyons,
lolls in sagebrush basins where snow geese ride pearl ponds.

A luminous bugle wakes Bosque del Apache creatures.
River of the Pueblos, of kit fox and bobcat,
of cottonwood, ash, and sycamore.
Map of God following no map, Rio Grande of deliverance.

Rio Grande of deliverance awaiting the beautiful doomed:
a Salvadoran boy runs past a field with his pup Pancho when MI8 surrounds him.
Join us! Clouds drift above Guazapa volcano, where the boy looks up,

waits. Their fists are hammers, a warning. Dog whimpers
in the boy's swollen arms. He runs that night, sobbing for Pancho,
for his own powerlessness, for a blue volcano, for abuelo's sorghum fields,
for the ten-hour walk ahead beneath a night of stars and prayer.

A night of stars beseeching Monseñor Oscar Romero.
Monseñor, Monseñor, whispered beneath a ceiba tree before sleep.
Monseñor into the smell of fumes and piss in a bus terminal.

Monseñor in an open truck switch-backing the Guatemalan altiplano,
Monseñor on a boxcar roof, clutching its ledge with boys in flight,
angels of the wretched, rocking past silver fields, wind in their black hair.
Monseñor at the Rio Grande, *ayudame!* as the boy wades in.

Ayudame Hermana, mothers whisper, their eyes darting
like hummingbirds, their children too quiet.
Yes, we Sisters offer towels, soap, rock the children

whose fevered eyes never leave the mother who held their hand
when Federales stole her savings, when she held them asleep on church steps,
when she begged. Their lives burning with each step toward
the Rio Bravo. What misery would you take for your children?

Yes, we have sheltered children on the misery road. Never this:
our own country trucking them, like cattle, back to slaughter;
the Americans jailing them—these anguished ones.

Yes, we have fed them whose suffering shames us.
These, whose hearts are pierced, who walk a shattered path,
their longing larger than danger.
Yes, they help us see reality through the eyes of God.

The eyes of God watch the river slip around Trini's body.
This last anointing where he floats ghostlike in a canal,
his feet and arms lashed in hydrilla weeds.

His eyes stare back at God.
A farmer from Ocotopecque, Trini left Honduran highlands
where cloud forests flash with blue-throated motmots;
where coffee leaves lift open palms, bracelets of red beans;

where coffee fields lie below fog-drenched cemeteries
with their gigantic dead; where Copan morgues overflow;
where Commissioner *El Tigre*'s death squads pile bodies like gladiolas.

Trini ran 1,500 miles from the blooming dead only to join
the drowned cadre of the Rio Grande—his sack of bones
in the migrant's cemetery is what is left of his one gamble.
Months or years from now his wife will light candles and call his name.

for Stephen Manning

Someday he will tell of the Family Detention Center
where he listened to sordid confessions, not of sinners,
but of victims—the raped, beaten, extorted, humiliated mothers.

Law—his authority, his compass, his weapon—
is a captive. Still he insists: *this mother, Your Honor,*
has met law's requirements for bond. Measured tone, reasonable.
Until Estrella, a four-year-old jailed with her mother for eight months.

After eight months, government attorney says: *What's so special about them?*
He turns the mask of his face away. Witness to her uncle's murder,
two rivers crossed, fevers, snakes, hunger, Estrella's childhood in a prison.

Estrella shows Stephen her jacket, yellow, blue stars of every size.
Which is your favorite? Points to the smallest star. Why so tiny?
Because it's the star over my heart. Her black curls bounce, she twirls.
Unbroken, shining. Stephen covers his eyes.

for Kenia Galeano

Unbroken, Kenia whispers to her boy, *you and I are unbroken.*
Yes, he saw me beg, saw my timidity, saw my humiliation.
But this American prison has turned him to silence.

I joined the hunger fast to give him words again.
Hijo, speak of this—our hunger and their power,
our suffering and their electronic doors. Seventy-seven of us
threatened with solitary if we don't eat.

Threatened with bread, we grow stronger. Son, scatter
this hunger as your brother threw seed into our blue-black field.
Remember him free, hijo, remember him before

the gang. What can I give you but this hunger
which does not belong to me but to all of us in this
place where no bells remember the hour, where tears
fill a cistern, where children lose voice.

for Noe and for Benny Martinez

In Brooks County, Texas, a smuggler abandons the boy.
Scorpions, diamondbacks, a white blaze on a sea of scrub brush.
Noe vomits, vomits. Forty miles from the Rio Grande, one thousand

from Usulatan where M13 killed his father. Noe whispers *Popi*
into a bloodred twilight. His last. Sheriff Benny Martinez carries
the boy's remains, shakes his head. Days of wild boars,
his sun-bleached skeleton white as snow. Martinez: *I'm sorry.*

He is sorry to be late, sorry the new Falfurrias checkpoint sends
them into a 940 square mile furnace, sorry he's become a curator of bones,
a gravedigger, a man who places faded rosaries, farewell letters in body bags.

Two hundred body bags in Sacred Heart Cemetery. Hundreds more out there
in sand sepulchers. Here is why Benny Martinez goes on—calls to his
dispatcher, terrible calls, sobs, voices from the almost dead—almost.
Martinez's deputies reach them, cradle them, save them. The living, the living.

LIKE A DOOR FLUNG OPEN

Beyond our sun, fourteen billion more suns

here, now a dark fan of geese, a tangerine dawn,
this donkey river carrying the flaming sky

this radiance

      oh see how we have no power here
no choice but to see this door flung open

our consent or sadness doesn't matter,

the river and bosque will be.
      Even if we sin against creation

cranes and kingfishers will lift from a river
      somewhere in a morning

      without us.

I see you grasp the child's hand, Elena,
the maize field falling lavender.
Silencio! you whisper. Two silhouettes

moving into shadows. You are
a gambler now, walking to America
with a knapsack of tortillas and boiled eggs.

You finger a medal of Madre de Dios
who knew about terror and invisibility.
You check the US dollars sewn into a skirt,

the paper with your cousin's Ohio address,
a vial of contraceptive pills. Ahead, moon shudders
on the path MI8 will follow, so you veer to river's cover.

A tiny strategist, you outwit the deadened boys
with black heart tattoos on bodies
that wait for the bullet prepared for them from birth.

In the 1980s, I knew your grandmothers,
campesinas whose children became ghosts,
los desaparecidos, whose tortured limbs

were dumped in mass graves, all that is sacred
hidden somewhere as you hurry through a land of bones
and its martyrs in the blue flame of evening.

Those mothers of the disappeared walked
through fire. I don't know what else I believed then
but I believed in them. That time outside

of time when catastrophe took me to the world
like a fist blow, a drowning, a birth.
I was never the same *gringa*. It is why I've come here,

Elena, to a South Texas detention center where you
and the exhausted boy at your side wait for deliverance.
It is recompense, what they lit in me

when they became flames, their fidelity
a brightness death could not extinguish.
It is all so distant, impossible. God did not embarrass them.

What do mystics say—if you want God, embrace
simplicity, lay down anxiety like a gun you are
pointing at your head. They spoke of God

like they would about new seed, a catechist dragged off,
the river rising—God with them, no filters.
Bodies everywhere. They held open wild blessed light.

Some of this I imagine, some of it was unimaginable.
You were not yet born when they gave themselves over
for the dream of you; for a small country of *veranera* bloom.

Now, you are targets of boys without mercy who
have received none. Festooned with death symbols,
they aim rage at each other, at you, at themselves,

a mad house where those who cannot pay the *renta*
run. The journey then where violation owns the crossroads.
Your boy's whimper when the Zetas took your savings,

when you gave the coyote the extra payment he demanded,
asking your child to wait in the field away from your humiliation.
Sun like a thug stalking you each day of sweat, thirst, hunger.

Fear of weakening, a threat you slice in two like a snake.
What spirit accompanied you when you stayed in a safe house
for six days with only mangoes for the boy,

when you pulled him up the bank at midnight,
his muddied feet slipping on the ground of freedom.
This rio, you said, *is the last, here we are safe.*

The Rio Grande looked away when searchlights burst.
It rolled on, having done its best to offer
its waters' ancient benediction.

Now America's welcome party and clean sheets.
Uniforms and barbed wire, guards and play schools
for profit. Karnes Detention Center terrified him.

Toy trucks, videos of kindly monsters, games—none of it
fooled the kid: *Mama, why do the police keep us here?*
You dream hooded vultures who wait for deportation planes

to touch down in *Ilopango* airport. They are hungry.
They can wait. They know you are coming back.
The night before your court case, your *abuela*

appears in a dream, tells you not to worry.
Next to her a judge with angel wings waves at you.
Trust which one? You are the granddaughter

of farmers who were realists. Against those
with AK47s, grenades, clandestine jails,
helicopters and B 57s, they bet on life
and on each other.

Go with *abuela's* assurance.
Her dream is your history.

LAMENT

Texas Detention Release House

I tell a Honduran mother shushing
four-year-old Luisa, *You are brave.*
Does her soul carry the mutilated road,
its shame a lost scripture written in dust?
Luisa's mother looks away from me.
Kids clutch teddy bears they'll kiss
good-bye, leave on windowsills.

Each mother wears an ankle bracelet
that announces them Job's daughter, too tired
to argue with God as they hike children onto
buses bound for Boston or Iowa.
They have signs: *I speak no English—*
which bus do I take next?

My grandmother appeared in my dreams:
We rattlebrained Bridgets, scrubbed brass,
toilets, became citizens, obeyed.
Kept the back door open for the others
seeking America on its terms—factory work,
and housekeeping. Outliers, yet we had
the keys to the kingdom: milky skin
and we knew the language of empire.

My grandmother never spoke like this.
In the dream she has joined Honduran mothers
carrying children across the Rio Grande.
The River Shannon was ours but could not save us.

My grandmother never saw the Texas border,
or families in federal detention. But it was her brogue
that I heard in the dream: *Pay heed. As for us—*
we hid our peoples' memories of death bells.
We survived.

The river of deliverance lies a thousand miles from Rosa's El Salvador.
       Before her mud-water baptism in the Rio Bravo
       she walks a *Via Dolorosa* of small deaths, her body

a wound, a target, an animal. Her four-year-old's
       cries cannot break her, *cannot.*
       Three tortillas for two days.

Alert for Zeta gang wolves, she wears dark clothes,
       a ball cap pulled low, huddles with other mothers,
       lambs who are their own shepherd.

Her arms ache gripping Carlos and the steel lip
       of the boxcar roof. There, facing wind's mercy,
       the boy's tears stop. He shouts, *cows, Mama, look.*

At Tenosique the train halts. Sun is a knife.
       Mothers, kids form a circle that tightens
       when a man pulls a wagon over the tracks

to begin pitching up cheese and bean tortilla wraps,
       plastic water bottles. He moves along boxcars
       to a chorus of blessings, tears, kids waving.

Bows. Leaves. Legend of the angel of Tenosique begins.

An exquisite compass, small as a butterfly heart,
light as breath, guides *las mariposas* as they
move like a sunset cloud,
holding the air gold all the way to Mexico—
if they avoid predators and cold,
if they catch good thermals,
if creatures that weigh a half gram
are not blown off course—then
they will pass through the needle
of the Rio Grande between Eagle Pass
and Del Rio, Texas.

Ragged, exhausted migrants
cross the river on wobbly rafts
to reach the safety of a chance—
if they are not killed by Zetas,
if they endure the scorch of Texas badlands,
if they are not arrested by Federales,
if their smuggler does not abandon them,
if they don't die of heat exhaustion,
if they don't cramp,
if they don't panic in river currents—
then, they will gain the opportunity
to clean toilets, make beds,
wash dishes, mow lawns and trim shrubs,
to live in the shadows,
to fear a knock on the door,
to hope their kids have a chance—
to be grateful.

When she could hide him no longer, she took for him a basket
made of bulrushes and daubed it with bitumen and pitch. She put
the child in it and placed it among the reeds by the river bank.
EXODUS 2:3

His bruised face, a scapular under his shirt
that did nothing to protect him from a beatdown.
She is done with pleading, done with her country.

Hijo, the second river is your deliverance, may angels carry you across.

He will walk the road of eyes that see in the dark.
He will carry a backpack of her *pupusas*
that will last three days. Outside, the moon
has pooled their fields gold brown as a river.

She knows his odds.

Here, she whispers to the hissing path, *bless him*.
She is ordained by this night's extremity,
her raised hands like small boats in a river.
She waits there in the thick perfume of evening,
asking heaven. This blessing of slaves,
of brokenhearted mothers. This boy's life.

NÁ GÉILL, NUNCA ABDICACIÓN
(NEVER SURRENDER)

1847

Where they swam near Matamoros, currents run sudden.
Boots tied on their necks, arms pull, pull toward

a fight that will be their choice. Not for American
Generals who despise Papists. Stubborn, Paddy soldiers

have deserted, gone to the priests' Mexican people,
to an ancient fluency with defeat and the plight of the aggrieved.

They had fled Connemara and Kerry on coffin ships,
left fields of heather and corpses. Gaelic grief made them brash.

They cannot name what they carry, an abandonment
so hidden and haunted. What allegiance can ever fill them?

On moonless nights, more swim to the Irish battalions
on the other side of the great river, a land of familiar chaos,

poverty, ghosts, and rosaries. The Irish are fierce artillerists
under a Mexican colonel and their own Captain John O'Reilly

even as General Winifred Scott advances from Vera Cruz
and Zach Taylor's dragoons cross the Rio Grande. Fluttering above

cannon smoke and shrieks, the San Patricios hold aloft a green silk flag
the nuns at San Luis Potosí embroidered with a gold harp,

shamrocks, and inscribed below in Irish and Spanish
erin go bragh! and *Libertad por la Republica Mexicana.*

At Churubusco the San Patricios shout *ná géill* at bluecoat swarm.
Ammunition exhausted, Mexicans and Irish unsheathe swords.

Outnumbered, the Irish rush the space left as if that were
their territory—the spaciousness of defiance that the colonized claim.

On Scott's orders, the San Patricios are to be hung publicly while watching
Mexico's flag sinking and the American flag rising. Fitting last blow.

Patricios, feet and hands bound, ropes on necks, cheer the Mexican flag.
America's flag rises in a strangled silence that envelops the vanquished air.

On Connemara bogland young John O'Reilly walked hungry;
in Doolough Valley the frail and dying scavenged until they became fog.

Irish music fell with their dead. Defeat silenced two peoples
who danced until they were ghosts.

Today, in a dappled Mexico City plaza, a plaque reads:
*To the San Patricio Battalion, martyrs who gave their lives for the cause
of Mexico.*

I taught English. José Luis taught me the Mexican
defeat at Chapultepec and *Los Niños Héroes*.
If his English halted, others called out in the victor's
language so their peoples' valor
would burn like monastery candles.

That class night, hotel maids, gardeners, factory
workers were not tired. They built a fortress
of words to tell of Mexico's fall to General Scott's
final advance on Chapultepec.

And to tell of the six teenage cadets
killed defending the castle of Chapultepec.

> *English, English, José*, I coached when he stumbled.

> *Boys, only boys, bombas everywhere, boom, boom.*
> *Americanos say! basta Mejicanos!*

> Transfixed, José Luis is there in 1847,
hears cannon blast pound the Citadel,
his hands speaking when English words are dead to him.
Mexicans have no more ammunition,
his hand makes a gun—*no bam! bam!*
Trapped, outnumbered—he backs into a corner.

> *!Imposible!*

> Someone shouts: *Americanos say surrender.*

> José Luis stands: *Little soldiers say, no, !nunca!*

Bluecoats with rifles enter the castle,
boys lift swords. José charges an invisible army.

Pure silence.

> I am *Juan Escutia.* José Luis wraps a coat around himself,
> says, *bandera.* Someone says:
> *One boy, Juan, covers himself with the Mexican flag.*

José stands on a chair now, wears the "flag," then jumps. He doesn't try
for language, wants me to see sacrifice, words are too burdened.

> The others finish, *then Juan leapt to his death.*

> *Bandera* is ours, *de los Americanos, nunca!* José Luis's voice is
hushed.

Applause. Year after year of fieldwork, NAFTA took their small plots,
wading the Rio Bravo for the dream of minimum wage, trailer parks,
their children's one chance.

That night, *memoria* burned luminous, dangerous.

VOWS

for Sister Norma Pimentel of the Rio Grande Valley

The fidelity of those carrying
children up from the river shames me.

We give hot soup, showers. We listen.

They whisper—*my boy, Sister, his body in a ravine.*
A Honduran mother confesses she could not save her
fourteen-year-old girl from gang rape.

Can I absolve them of powerlessness?
Can I absolve *la migra* who don't make the laws?
Can I absolve the comfortable?
Can I absolve myself, my vowed, safe life?

This Rio Grande Valley holds the evidence.
Cracked boots bleached grey; tiny muddied tennis shoes.
Shirts stained with sweat, dust, stink of the river.

Brownsville neighbors say
Why, Sister, why must we save them?
Think of your house on fire.
Think of a firing squad.
Think of a hanging tree.

We Texans—who mark our lives in dawns
without a door kicked in—
we are a boat, we are the river, we are deeper now.

What would you do to save your children?
What vows would you keep?
What vows would you break?

I asked a deaf Navajo girl who signed *toohnilini*, river,
I asked a six-year-old Honduran gripping a boxcar ladder,
I asked a border guard who held night in his eyes,
I asked Hermana Rosita who lacked enough medicines,
I asked a *gringo* lawyer who cursed the law,
I asked a coyote who left them at the river, *Suerte*,
I asked José who lost a leg on *La Bestia*,
I asked a mother who dug her boy's grave,
I asked a judge with cinder eyes,
I asked the president who could not remember,
I asked MI8 who no longer recognized themselves,
I asked a boy carrying his brother's decayed body from the wild boars
and coyotes of Brooks County,
I asked a rancher who gave them water,
I asked America.

My beloved Maggie trotted the Rio Grande
path looking for me. I ran a mile, breathless along
the river's woody banks, panicked, gasping.

My mother lost my dog Scruffy in 1985 while I was in El Salvador.
I returned carrying the terrible grief of mothers of the disappeared.

In the presence of such inexpressible loss, how could I grieve?

But I did. My mother thought Scruffy fell through lake ice.

Maggie was ahead running for me, I was running for Maggie, shouting her
    name,
        losing breath.

I never saw my mother panic even when her failing lungs could not take in
    air.

You have to let me go, she said. Was I letting Maggie go, my own
lungs exploding? The river was turning dark, a tremble of stars.

The river's grief too.

My mother slid down the wall unable to find air.

I could not catch my dog or my breath.

TONY AND THE RIO GRANDE

He swims at times . . . down the Rio Grande
with students who will become like him elements/particles . . .
the river flowing forever.
TONY MARES

Some lessons are dark baptisms
from a teacher who had faith,
not in religion, but in vastness that pulls us
like the river to an unknown sea.
He believed, too, in his ancestor's land
where Mexican ghosts harvested corn and chile;
a teacher with trust in waters that carried
the story of *los invisibles*.

The professor was young and intense.
The ancient river still strong. Near sunset
river's mud-brown mirror was dappled magenta.
He said *Vengan, mis estudiantes,*
dive with me into our history deeper than books.
They swam past silver and violet eddies.
Stroke, stroke beneath lost light, a rise of stars.

The river knew him when he was three years old,
how the slow swirl took him down
until his father dove for his thrashing baby fish.

Like his father, the man whispered to anyone
drowning, *take my hand*.

WITHOUT A COMPASS

The river is embedded in God.
LI-YOUNG LEE

I walk a bosque trail at dawn.
Dark crowns of trees are fire gold.
Frog bassoon, ducks' tiny silver quakes.

What beauty slows us, what flash,
flutter, shimmer, blue dust,
tail flick in dark waters
snuffs our noise?
To listen, listen to
    cottonwood's tambourines.

If we are still.

So much is alive here, river's voice—
carried from ice, its operatic plunge,
an aria sung through canyon and desert
to join the Gulf coast's vast, roiling hymn.

Bones in this watershed
rest in sand and mud, beasts and birds
who fell like stars into darkness.
Ancient Pueblos' bones lie deep
and scarred, an indictment
the air and trees hold in flames.
Stones in the river protrude like ribs.

Still I walk in God's company
without a compass
listening to the river's trees.

CHICAGO—ILLINOIS RIVERS

THE QUESTION

From my moonlit porch bed on Dante Street, I heard
a train rumble our star-dazzled prairie. I was eight,

adrift in the night music, a dog barking in the distance.
My uncles had no war injuries. I had no questions for God.

But then Sister Mercedes told us a story.
Two boys were playing in boxcars, she began.

Mortality floated into the classroom
like the angel of death. I held

my breath. *When the train lunged it slammed the door
on one boy's head. His friend cradled him, children.*

He said the Act of Contrition with his dying friend.
On my way home, I walked past Kelly's store

but did not buy one penny candy, walked past
victory gardens and did not check my carrots.

I saw the boy choking on his last prayer,
blood staining his friend's shirt. I saw him die,

and I did not care about forgiveness or sins.

                             After that, I was late
for everything: dinner, mass, piano practice.

I arrived at school after the bell, fumbling
a lunchbox with a faded Dumbo,

my fat notebook spilling sheets of the wrong
assignment. I knew my mother had no answer

and I'd been given a grief that changed
the solace of night outside my porch window.

My manifesto of inchoate refusals:
I will barely show up; I will not be on the right page;

I will keep my question.

THE LEAP

1995, Darien, Illinois

When the duck arrived on her balcony
my mother became an unbidden
midwife for the brown-grey muff of feathers
that sat on her eggs, still as a decoy.

Five stories below, a pond of reeds and green muck.
Woodland swamps and the river canal farther south.
The duck preferred high blue safety for the nest.
Took the gash of wind, rain drumming.

The pond at night a house of noise, frog *basso profundo*
from that island of moonlight.

Spring light everywhere, forsythia waving yellow gloves.
My mother lay near the porch window, conscious still.
                    Her body, the sheets, luminous in sunlight.

The priest came, and my sister and I gathered her. She wanted
that—to sit up. He gave us oil to anoint her. The blue eyes
paler and paler. Below, geese slid into dark waters like tiny
acolytes in a liturgy of flight and descent.

For weeks my mother watched the eggs, keeping her distance.
She worried, knew the treachery of hawks, any birth a gamble,
hurling new beauty into the world with all your strength,
never sure if the tiny one will take to the blue air.

My mother didn't see them hatch in the hours before dawn.
She knew they had twenty-four hours to get to water.
Fluff balls who would follow off a precipice,
one after another fluttering down like yellow stars.

Soon my mother watched the ducklings waddle,
then swim in and out of the brown cigars of cattails.

This Alleluia! amid the pond traffic of emerald-
capped mallards and geese with their dark monk cowls.

The priest said, *I have come to bless you as you have blessed
others*, as if care is a cliff we walk day after day
until we leap to air and ash.

My mother lifted her head that last time.

Thank you, she said.

A loop of blue barn swallows coasts high
above Chicago in lightless air, hidden in the hour
between night and dawn.

Before Michigan Avenue Bridge freezes over,
the birds will leave like Irish travelers without notice,
haul for Argentina or Uruguay beating on sky roads,
jabs of rain, catching rides on thermals.

My grandfather watched gannets
careen above the Queenstown steamer
leaving Cobh harbor, his last sight of Ireland.
Then he turned to watch gulls, blue emptiness.

In May, chimney swifts and nighthawks
drop off Lake Michigan winds, acrobats
in dark light, riding out of eyesight, camouflaged,
their plumage sepia as predawn, silhouettes
with twenty-three-inch wingspreads scissoring.
So high and mimetic, they are invisible.

MAGICIANS

1836, Illinois and Michigan Canal

We come from Connemara farmers
who carried stone to the sea; our arms
broke bog's rock doors.

This is the river we Paddies turn
toward the great Mississippi.
Our arms slice prairie, hardpan, and black root.

We, the anonymous, caked in dirt.
Bruised hands gut meadows of canary weed,
sedge marsh alongside dark men with scarred

backs, lashed by a deeper servitude.
Together worn down, our shoulders cramped.
We open thirty miles of glacial till,

men, as taken for granted as this canal
turned backward, pierced with locks
and pumping stations. Our young lives

save a city from typhoid, make a way through
bedrock. We magicians do not
attend the "shovel-day" opening.

We are the nameless, who made
a silver highway for freight boats
pulled along towpaths by mules like us.

WHATEVER YOU SAY, SAY NOTHING

Seamus Heaney

For Maggie O'Connell Golden

Maggie arrived in Chicago's bully hour
with nothing to match its glare.

Her floppy wool hat announced old country.
Union Station was a merry-go-round of Yanks

in dark suits whirling past the sixteen-year-old.
America, she saw, rode a fast horse.

Maggie stood stiff among strangers shooting past,
gripped her suitcase as an anchor.

Alert for her sister Katy's brogue—calling
Maggie, Maggie as if something had ended.

Maggie had left Caherciveen and the weedy coast
where her distant relative, the great Dan O'Connell's

Derrynane, stood imperious, a smoke-stone great house
that faced the bay's sand paths at Ireland's edge.

Derrynane, below Macgillicuddy's Reef where, across
three heathered fields of matted sheep, stood Maggie's cottage

that held her O'Connells who slept with goats in two rooms.
Her father, Michael, in the salted air of farmland

heaved sod from rock soil as if time were a landlord.
If her quiet father complained, Maggie and her sisters

remembered little, so erased were their own worries.
What voice would Maggie bring if not the voice

of women who owned nothing, not land,
nor history, the property of defiant orators and rebels?

Maggie's American home was devoid of Celtic symbols
as if she forgot or carried her first lesson—

silence and invisibility. No Irish knot symbols,
announcing her country, herself.

There was Irish women's art: Maggie's crocheted lace doilies
lay on armrests intricate as large snowflakes.

Maggie gave six children the soul-gift of kindness
and the talisman of quiet and courtesy.

Whatever you do, make no fuss.

LAMBS OF GOD

2017, St. James churchyard on a bluff above the Calumet Sag

Rest now, Irish diggers, who linked the waters.
Rest, brawny priests changing the elements,
spinning this canal to grand passage.

Your bones lie close to a river of reed
and mud threading toward vastness,
toward a confluence that cannot stay, a river
of perpetual good-byes. You are self-forgetful,
staked here in an abandoned cemetery
on a field of tall grass brittle
with pale ice, wind, and silence.

Snow falls on stone markers, over
the abandoned limestone church
where you sang *Angus Dei*, not to ask
for forgiveness—you expected little—
but for peace from the demon drudgery.

You who believed in the river's glory,
in engineers' astonishing calculations.
Your own beauty obliterated winter after winter.

Where the river passes below, black maple leaves
are flung like work gloves.

FOULED

1885

The girl's chest rises faint as a robin's,
her breath slipping. Her mother wrings

a compress, carries it to the pale child
whose eyes flutter, ready for flight.

In the alley, men hammer coffins, break silence
with a pitiful repetition of nail hits and coughs.

Women keep watch, finger their beads. The mother
wails. Outside, tenement clotheslines sag

with rags that did no good. The river is a dog
reeking with mange but no one helps,

no one knows how typhoid runs
its death wagon through the neighborhoods.

Those who will save the city from a river emptying
sewage into Lake Michigan are coffin makers

who will lay their children down, who will dig
through hardpan, bust limestone and mud walls,

who will blast, cut, smash, carry rock
to hoppers for four years. Burly surgeons will

cut a twenty-eight-mile incision to reverse the river's flow,
build sluice gates, thirty-one bridges, and locks

to insist the river backward to the Mississippi.
Immigrants with caked hands who will wave caps

when the water breaks through like a sinner
who repents.

2017

If there are angels they love
this grubby river, once pure green road

that carried missionaries and madmen.
Acrobat river twisted backward, sullied

with butcher's rump and entrails, a mule river,
mistreated, bent. Yet its steady pull, like distant

bells, invites angels, a procession of ducks
in dawn's russet-gold morning.

An old man pitches a grist of stale
bread to tiny river monks.

Two Labs lunge gorgeously as if air
might suspend them, paws splayed out,

trusting the river's mint carpet.
Beavers slip-slide off sepia banks

into the slow waltz of geese and egrets.
An intonation rises, a chorus of juncos,

wrens, chickadees.

If I tell you this river is a slow god
lolling toward tall grass, savannas' long
stations of burr oak, of sassafras-leafed sun
below the silence of clouds, of stars
over bluegrass, the prairie deep, asleep;
if I tell you the river is up all night

rocking the land to quiet, a night-
light of moon to guide geese to sleep.
Deer drink dark rose water before sun,
before a cry of geese trumpeting long.
If I tell you the river is a brown god
who carries turtles and snails and stars,

would you place her in the pantheon of stars?
Where we paddled past blue heron in sun,
past meadows of phlox and buttercup, long
shrub barrens of hazelnut until we came to sleep
near the river's voice murmuring to night.
The lull like a distant bell, the beckons of a god.

If I tell you the river is a circus god,
a ballet of swimmers each night.
Our own two voices quieter, untroubled in the long
prayer of prairie and river answering stars
while rock bass, trout, beaver, badger sleep.
With first light, the stage belongs to red sun.

I tell you we stroked, stroked into late sun
riding the Calumet to the Des Plaines, stars
falling as we paddle the Illinois, a shatter of long
diamond tails. In the distance, coyotes announce night.
We ride solemn in a procession toward God.
So much of our time lost, asleep.

This trail of Marquette, who did not sleep,
followed Potawatomi braves beneath a spring sun
that could not warm him. Now we paddle toward night,
brave or cowardly, beneath a bowl of stars.
Each dip and pull a test that we practice long
on the back of an ancient brown god.

Sun's long adieu, the hush of night.
We pull, pull against sleep, river a cistern of stars.
What canticle is praise enough for this strolling god?

1675
His shoulder muscles tight, then loose. In February,
hands blue on the paddle. In April, his group passes
swans, sand hill cranes with red eyebrows, a prairie
of rose phlox, riffs of purple blazing stars, all so pure

that Marquette whispers a glory canticle
from the Book of Daniel: *Benedicite opera Domini, Domino.*
Blessing given, received. Even now,
stroking into green-blue hours,

the priest is deathly ill but he says nothing.
Illini Indians glide Jacques past cattails, indigenous disciples
who believe the dead surround us, that wolf and hawk
spirits come to the broken, that we meet

spirit here, only here beneath dogwood, hickory,
hornbeam, and black maple trees. Here where we lie
in prairies of evening primrose, swaths
of lady's slippers, purple joe-pye weed.

This beauty abounding, not another world of Christians.
Yet the Illini have come for Jacques because he believes
in them, because his God favors the hungry. Did Jacques
grip the paddle tightly to bless pain, to tell the river

his perfect weakness, each stroke an absolution?
Fearless now, because he forgot himself long ago,
he watches Easter break open tiny yellow buds, winces
as he paddles and receives the river's last blessing.

CHIEF SHABBONA'S VISION

He fought them, men the color
of clouds. Rock River whispered:

remain, remain. The land's voice:
thrushes, blackbirds, snowy owl,

its body a tattoo of wild indigo, jewelweed.
Each season told Potawatomi who to become,

how dawn and starlight gave heart
as if the prairie made them,

offered itself, in howl and hoot,
in stillness and white frost.

He fought them with Tecumseh
until his people's blood and theirs

became a stream they could not cross,
could not staunch, could not bear.

He laid down defiance
as a warrior who saw

their dreams and knew
defeat. Shabbona swallowed

the bitter drink of wisdom;
he warned Potawatomi,

warned white settlers,
warned Indians that loss

comes early like snow,
covers rows of the dead.

JEAN BAPTISTE POINT DU SABLE'S PATIENCE

founder of Chicago

Who loved him taught him to wait.

His Haitian slave mother read oceans,
watched all signs of freedom rise
and crash like tropical waves.

His beloved Kihihawa bride believed
in the scripture of elk, rabbit, and Jesus;
believed, dangerously, in American patriots.

At River du Chemin, British soldiers encircled
his cabin, their jackets, fire red, ignited the air.
He knew their danger, knew their language,
knew four Indian dialects, knew French
and Spanish, knew he would outsmart them,
knew they knew.

A rebel sympathizer, jailed one year,
he knew how to wait and whom to trust—
Blacks, Indians, trappers, a French Jesuit.

His own wits taught him fur trade and French art;
Thomas Paine taught him who would win.
At the river's mouth, gulls loop above Lake Michigan

where, surrounded by bean fields, du Sable's cabin
sat like an altar facing the spirit of waters.
At night he watched the moon pearl the lake
like a god strewing flowers. Next to his

homestead, the river's slow elephant plod, passed.
Patience, the river whispered, *patience*.

WHAT DO WE KNOW

OF THE LAWS AND CUSTOMS

OF WHITE PEOPLE?

Blackhawk, Sauk Chief

Rock River's low fluting whistle
where wind rocked cornfield's green cradle.

What Blackhawk loves, he will lose:
you touched the goose quill to the treaty

not knowing you consented to give away
your village which lies now rotted,

corpse fields wave flags of stubble,
a defeat the land endures impatient

as your river that wants wind and
an open run, cannot hold back.

Whites, with quill pens that pierce, order you to loss
upon loss. Ponies, stallions, grandmothers,

babies into the great river to a land
they call Iowa, your people driven like buffalo.

You touched the goose quill to the treaty
not knowing you consented.

⁓

Black Hawk War, 1832

In the green hour, yellow star grass, meadowlark,
your land calls in the blue work of dawn.

At Yellow Banks, two thousand warriors swim like otters,
silent, muscled, invisible into the Mississippi current.

At Dixon's Ferry you know your fate:
Potawatomi, Winnebago

brothers will not rise.
Major Stillman advances now; a descent

of ravens darkens sky and prairie.
Three warriors carry your white flag. Wind furls

the banner; their hands tremble where
they grip. Stillman's militia trembles too—fires.

It is only beginning. Blackhawk begs river's deliverance.
At the Mississippi, doom opens its door,

a gunboat turns into position, aims upriver.
Blackhawk surrenders to draw bluecoats' mercy.

Moonlight opens the river's dark path,
offers thrashing Indians to them. Volley again and again.

Dead ponies and children in bright eddies.
Stroke after stroke amid the dead and drowning.

You *touched the goose quill . . . not knowing.*

UNION STOCKYARDS

I

1910

My grandmother, Maggie, hears the Yard's bellow.
Dying squeals, all the way to Sangamon Street.

Her Richard is a young worker who daily stands
in two inches of burgundy water.

In winter his hands are mottled blue and purple.
He hacks entrails for twelve slimed hours.

Shoulders swollen and tight. A bronchial cough.
He can't miss a shift this side of heaven.

They salvage: guts for violin strings,
soap, glue, buttons, leather shoe polish,

fertilizer, and perfume. This, my pig body,
this, my cow blood, given.

Entrails and guts are thrown into the river until
the offal brews, bubbles and bubbles.

Chicago River takes gaseous sewage
like a helpless beast smelling its own death.

II

Katy and I at Bubbly Creek One Hundred Years Later

My sister navigates our canoe along the gritty south branch
toward the Southeast side of our baptisms.

At the wide turning basin we pull instead
toward our father's old neighborhood where the river

ran to the stockyards, a dog making its last run.
It is late afternoon, September sun scarlet against

banks of box elder and cottonwood. We watch egrets
ride below high tables of urban buildings, the skeleton

Yards too high to see above bulrush. My sister directs
a turnabout, her red-blonde hair aflame in slanting light.

Around us, like a low boiling stew, hundreds
of bubbles. We ride quiet, held by waters

that mark history with methane. Above,
in gathering shadow, the great slaughterhouse

monument to Chicago's rise, silent at last.

The ghost of Haymarket is always here.
                                    Studs Terkel
November 11, 1887

Yes I have come for Albert's hanging,
eyes to bear his torment.
My silence a last farewell
when the hood slips on.

      But Albert will die without us.
          Yes, I bring little Albert and Lulu,
              their small hands trembling in mine,
                their bird hearts banging.

Yes, police shove us in a dank cell
as if grief could burn through walls,
ignite this city.

Outside the crowd's roar,
a slam when the release drops.

      A dark bird flutters in my chest.
      Lulu cries *Papa, Papa.*

Mercy is a candle snuffed.
I want a prairie fire that Inspector Bonfield
can't put out. I want a rising
Marshall Field can't buy.

        You'd refuse tears to save your
        children. You'd read Albert's letter
        to his babies. You'd do it. You'd do it.

Oh my children, how deeply your Papa loves you.
Remember one who dies not alone and for you,
but for the children yet unborn.
Bless you my darlings!

The bird is in my throat clawing.
Police say I am *more dangerous than a thousand rioters.*
This pleases me, a small brown woman
who knows how to write, speechify . . . to die.

After Lulu died, my troubled boy gave grief
and rage his own hanging rope.

Oh misery! I have drunk the cup of sorrow
to its dregs. But I am still a rebel.

Bonfield's boys follow me, arrive at union halls
and rallies like suitors who pull arrest warrants
like bouquets from their pockets. Snatch my pamphlets,
quick as terriers. I write for the silenced—*tramps,*
the unemployed, the disinherited, for porters
in Pullman's perfect city, workers in the Yards,
in McCormick's Harvester plant.

I am not fearless. I am bereft. I am on fire.

They lurk in hall shadows, disguised as tattered men,
wool caps pulled low, eyes like crows.
Oh it's danger, my companion. Come then,
we know this dance. You with your blackjack
two-step, me with a heart of stone.

Everything I touch burns. Emptiness is dry wood.
I salute the mothers who scavenge, the shutout fathers
who quiet their hollow-eyed children.

New order: I'm forbidden to speak on any Chicago street.
Our comrades wink, line the Chicago River. I wear
my taffeta dress, bow at the neck, step up on deck.
Paupers, rebels, ragged children cheer, wave
wool caps, flags; some run to keep up with a floating barge.

> *You must no longer die and rot in tenement houses . . .*
> *Shoulder to shoulder with one accord you should rise.*

1934, Bug House Square

No one knows me now, stepping shakily
onto a soapbox. I no longer see faces
or the green canopy shading the Square.

> *Just turn me toward the people,*
> *I've seen enough anyway.*

Long past my bright hours and Wobbly glory,
long past dreams of a rising,
long past Albert's last words
and my children's broken hearts,
long past May Day when workers
wrestled time from the clock keepers,
gave it, like bread, to the weary,
long past the cost of an eight-hour day,

I burn on, I burn.

WHITE CITY

1893, World's Columbian Exposition

What of risings from ash, what of a city with burnt wings?
This is stubborn Chicago, architects who slap

down blueprints like pugilists, dare any taker
to say impossible. So it lifts, this elegant White City

on planks over mud fields. Its glory falls like sunlight
over the Yard's blood pens where immigrants stand in muck

and gut-smeared boots, proud of the reflected grandeur
that rains like silver dimes over the tenements,

factories, and the sick river. Ida B. Wells is not proud
of the spectacle. She hands out photos

of lynchings in the magnolia-fragrant South
to the silk-hat and hoop-skirt tourists, who drop

the pamphlets in pavilion canisters.

This is our phoenix hour, the once scorched city
now a bellow of white luminosity: Venetian canals,

African savannas, Bordeaux and Limoges alabaster cathedrals.
We are cosmopolitan, we walk a promenade

past milk-white Baroque facades, we look up
to the Statue of the Republic gazing into pink and violet

waters, we hear the Mormon Tabernacle Choir sing.
On the Midway Plaisance we watch Harry Houdini

slip away like a Lake Michigan wave; on George Ferris's
264' bicycle-wheel-in-the-sky we watch the Fair

lanterns glimmer, and from this height we remember.

SS EASTLAND CAPSIZES
IN THE CHICAGO RIVER

1915

The Bridge Tender

My hand to bridge levers, at the ready, as I watched
men's white straw hats, the women's brimming
with pink and fuchsia flowers, boarding. Light dappled
the ship rails, winked in the river. Ready, I raised the bridge.

Then, not like the Titanic's hours of listing,
the boat dropped, a leopard taking a bullet.
Bodies flew like dolls, screams I still hear,
the river waked, upchucking baskets, toys, hats.

I slammed a lifeboat into the wild water.
I, a gray-haired man, found a crack in time, a door to heaven:
I pulled them like a Hercules into the boat gasping.
I rowed to the dock, the dead floating like wedding flowers around us.

The Police Diver

What held me, a diver weighted against river's chokehold when through my
helmet's tiny window of green blackness—I saw a band of angels turning in
circles—weightless white dresses, a girl with a yellow hair bow, boys in knickers
whose young mother was freight I pulled toward the dock, and although I held
her child I couldn't yank the line again, I became the father who tried to swim
past the ship's collapsed port side but could not find the surface, a black wall
pressing, the limp boy drifting, so I held him even though I could not signal,
and around me, bodies and more bodies against the line that ties us to safety:
a summer day, picnics, a band playing on the deck, a small hand in mine, a line
that kept me blessed, a line of breath that stakes us to the world. Alarmed, they
pulled me up. I never went down again.

Young Diver

I dove without helmet
or line into the hull
jagged as an open can,
carried up the girls of summer,
long skirts fluttering like clouds,
exposing their legs.
Onlookers shouted,
"Your lungs will burst."
I was seventeen and prince of the river
carrying the breathless
to the useless air.
I dove again and again
until twilight swept the sky purple.
I had borne forty bodies in my arms,
once a mother embracing her baby.
Bodies bobbed up.
Men used grappling irons
and pike poles to pull them out.
I lifted crates off bodies,
ripped away snagged cloth
and cradled them as if they knew me,
were my mother or father,
these loved or unloved strangers
I could not save.

A LINE BREAKING: 1919 RIOTS

I

July 27, 1919

Ninety-five degrees, wet, breathless air. Boy lifts
onto the raft, splashes. He watches the shore,
turns to check the raft's drift because he is
a black boy, because the lake cannot be his,

because the city cannot be his, because he must
watch the lines that hold him, pitiless.
The rock-thrower's aim is perfect. Boy's head
snaps back and he tumbles into summer waters,

a stain where he goes down. Like storm clouds,
thousands on 29th Street Beach. Their voices,
kept in the bell jars of blues, crack the glass.
From Bridgeport, white gangs come with tire irons

and baseball bats. Brownsville children sleep in closets;
their sweat-drenched fathers load army pistols.
Every window lightless, ready. At first stars, pale riders
advance with petrol under club jackets.

One hundred fire alarms. Smoke snuffing
out air like an altar boy extinguishing candles.
Suffocation, one way or another. Rumors, of black
bodies in the Chicago River, float like ash.

II

Rainbow Beach, 1960

Velma Murphy Hill links her arm, trembles.
A ribbon of dark young bodies wade in, hum
"We Shall Overcome." On shore watching,
a cinch of whites, the grandsons of 1919.

Blacks sing, tighten arms, walk into a history—
of no protection from rocks, punches—that they will own.
Velma Murphy Hill takes seventeen stitches.

The next year, one hundred process past beach enforcers
into a communal baptism—and it is sacramental
when they lock arms with white race traitors, march out dripping.

STEEL MILLS

The familiar blue smoke rose from mills
where iron bubbled in white-hot cauldrons.

Our fathers poured the gold like priests
transubstantiating molten for the world's architecture.

The Calumet River carried it all, the goods and the spillage.
Herons lifted above blast furnaces, pig iron and coke plants.

We cut lilies of the valley from the banks
for Mother's Day. Each morning when we crossed

crimson-licked fields, the men were already filing into
the plant's send-up of machine roar and girder clang

where they risked limbs for the purchase
of a southside bungalow. Men whose

blunt fingers played accordions in Polka bands,
blues harmonicas at Theresa's Club,

bodhran and fiddle at O'Halloran's,
whose hands worked shearing machines,

flywheels, cooling beds, gear boxes.
Then it was over. Men left enormous vats,

quenching boxes, adamite rolls, transporters,
to shadow and rust: America's rust belt cemetery.

Below Fisk Station coal stacks,
    a river rolls grey and joyless
        until 18th Street:
            guitars and violins call
                the dead with *corridos.*

Ancestors hover in wings of light,
descend like *mariposas* on trumpets,
on gold embroidered sombreros wide as crows' wings.

Mariachi's boot heels tap, tap
        in the footsteps of ghosts who carry
           marigolds in bony hands.

     Come skeletons with white rib cages
     and florescent leg bones, red flowers.

The dead whisper: here we are close as breath,
a cloud of witnesses whistling.

This neighborhood of *gritos*
      where they carry the Virgin,
          a goddess who wears a cloak of stars
             because the moonlit sky was a cosmos
                she and Juan Diego did not fear—a vision
                  ever ahead of what can be measured.

What purity of heart . . . a farmer who trusted
          a Maria who loves tattoos, gold teeth, platform shoes,
           remembers the souls of troubled boys,
              their *abuelas* holding broken hearts like
  fireballs.

Do you remember crossing the Michigan Avenue
Bridge, hefting a ratty copy of the *Summa Theologica,*

which proved nada as far as you were concerned? If I watched
the river below I'd be late for class but knew that God

did not need proofs, that time, like the river, altered every
route and could not belong to philosophy majors

drowning in gravitas, reading Camus who spat upon
proofs. Why didn't we read Levinas or Etty Hillesum

who couldn't get rid of God? In the Nazi camps, the sacred was
everywhere you looked, eyes haunted, imploring.

I can see us hurrying past the water tower, your scarf
flung over a secondhand tweed jacket, a battered briefcase

bulging with Sartre and books from Paul Carroll's class whom
we loved because he sat cross-legged on top of his desk, recited

Eliot, then fell quiet staring out the filthy windows toward the lake.
We loved the drama. I was looking for answers, not romance.

It has been fifty years. Long gone is the grungy student union
basement where we sat for hours in gray curls of smoke, seeking

an end to confusion like a barge captain who watches for sandbars
and currents, ever shifting just below.

How transitory each journey, how everything moves on. The river's
holy art, ancient and ever running.

I read Thomas Merton who pointed beyond the self, beyond language—this was as close to ancient wisdom as I could get. It was, is, unruly.

Who was I when I saw the world like a misty river, arrows of light breaking through?

BAPTISM

I returned to the Chicago River a diver,
someone who underwent God.

Swimmer, go deeper, deeper into silence.
Forget your given name, that person

who took up space and comfort—entitled,
who did not pass the potatoes mindful of others,

who finally grasped the ladder of simplicity.

After Compline I stood before a twilight canopy
lifting above a Swanton Ohio schoolyard

where I taught seven-year-olds to read.
The children of farmers taught me to listen—

night's low hum, last murmurs in barns.
I was nineteen, a postulant, dressed in black

like a mafia widow or an Amish buggy rider.
Not yet a real nun, I amused the children.

On Saturday I taught catechism in a clapboard church
where the children brought their dogs

who sat beneath oak trees but trotted in to check.
I redundantly taught catechism's rules of the origin

of everything to cocreators who helped their fathers
ignite the early green flares of cornfields in confederacy

with sun and rain. The God of catechism so puny.
The abundance trembling outside that paint-blistered

church door so blinding and sacred.

> Q. What is God?
> A. God is a spirit infinitely perfect.
> Q. Had God a beginning?
> A. God had no beginning.
> Q. Where is God?
> A. God is everywhere.
> Q. How many kinds of Baptism are there?
> A. There are three kinds: Baptism of water,
> of desire, and of blood.

I was water, blood, desire. I was alive in a time of apple blossom
and manure, of dogwood and snake rows of coiled black soil.

I believed, as confident as the woman at the well.
The kids and I, we believed anything was possible,

we believed we were accompanied by a presence
as loyal as their farm dogs.

In the white habit of a Dominican I walked weeping city streets.
My own heart ready, naïve, the world thrown up in chaos.

Dominican life was a wave that carried me
into Detroit's gathering storm.

The children's voices drowned my complaints.
Sixty black first graders taught me to dance,

and when their mothers asked me to march
after King's assassination, I knew my stroke

was strong enough. I dove in, swam—
just before Detroit burned.

I left behind the sacred rule, a floor-length
mohair habit and poise.

I-94 was the green road back to Chicago;
every tree waved. What I left, never left me.

In Chicago I walked with the weary, the militant,
the forsaken, who took my hand, an apprentice

in the rising flood of their dissent.

BLOOD RED

March 24, 1986

Back from El Salvador with no language for what we've seen.
How much silence is needed to keep the story far, far away?

We have only a gesture. But it is more than words:
a crew of religious navigators who don't know how

to paddle but are done praying. We portage canoes
down the riverbanks in the blue stillness before dawn.

Above us taxi lights bob across Michigan Avenue Bridge
oblivious of the brazen silhouettes below.

The river will have to mark the anniversary of Oscar Romero,
Bishop of the poor, assassinated because he feared

not the silence of the dead but the silence of the living.

Speak river, disturb us with your open wound
even if for a day.

⸻

Five a.m. The priest signals and three figures throw
dye into the river, their gloves stained scarlet.

Dawn's gold cup pours into the river's darkening red.
A minister moves from shadows, grips the gunwale,
lowers the canoe into bruised waters.
Downriver two nuns and a rabbi shove off,

paddle toward the third canoe where a Salvadoran
missionary and a pacifist priest dip and pull

through burgundy waters, hold signs,
US OUT OF SALVADOR, until cops arrive.

Bullhorns: *you will return to the dock.*
Even the canoes are arrested.

THERE IS NO DEAL

2017

I stand on the Montrose bridge, watch
a canoe upstream, sparks where paddles
dip, then pull through orbs of darkness.

Canoeists are confident that the river owes them
a ride to the mouth where canopied banks
are muscled out by warehouse girders,

transport docks, boatyards. Chicago's back door
still open for riffraff industrial parks, hurdy-gurdy
of shipyards and scrap metal, workers who

rarely go downtown where the city dwarfs
the river with empire's skyscrapers
competing like Icarus for the sun.

The river takes its time curling past the Merchandise Mart,
the Opera House, then turns south to abandoned mills
and glue factories. Grit and guts South Branch,

a draft horse plodding past swamp, sedge flats, cattails, reeds
of canary grass, tussock clumps. This river is its own myth,
refuses our interrogation, offers neither absolution nor blame.

Like an abused horse, she takes us on her back once more.
And like God, the river makes no deals.
What is given is given freely.

They have been swimming for years
silver and fat, gulping everything
until they can leap beyond themselves,
beyond breath, into a brightness
that pierces them as if for moments
they meet God who kisses them,
but if they linger
in their spinning jump they will
die of God, of blue dangerous air.

If startled, they fly from the river
eight feet into sky. Is it a defiance
or a demonstration of their fate,
these bully swimmers who devour
plankton, eat their way to eminence
—yet are destined for pain when they hit
the electric fences that punish them
away from the great lakes.

Thirty-seven miles from Chicago's watershed,
they are coming, a team of acrobats
with pink mouths as big as fists.

IN SPITE OF DEBRIS, OFFAL, TRASH, DETRITUS

A miracle of goldfish still flickers like
sunlit coins through dark matter.

This river asks for so little,
sings beneath Bascom bridges.
It's Prairie Wolf Slough's *Gloria*

of marsh marigold, pale geranium,
trout lily, swamp buttercup.

Clothed in its liquid vestment,
a raiment where deer and fox
drink and mark the hours.

    A river that remembers
    vast woodlands, meadows
    flaming in the silence marking time.

    This is the otter's prayer,
    a ballet of plunges and dives.
    The mallard's dark procession

on silk waters, then sudden flight
across dawn's flare where sky holds
them to perfect blue roads.

    They do not see the presence that enfolds
    them, so intimate their animal trust.

WHAT THE RIVER SAID

I spoke to the Chicago River today the way
I talk to God. Not begging. Grateful
as Potawatomi mothers dipping water gourds

in dawn light, a nod to thank the river.
Who, what were you, I asked the river,
when you were tribal, pure, a companion?

Silence, like God's, not even a whisper.
We came with muskets, then shovels, then dynamite.
I asked forgiveness. The dog we kids let out

near traffic. Its hind legs crippled.
This mutt river wounded with sewage,
oil, crop poison. Same sorrow.

———

In late spring, trees overhang the banks,
billows of lime-green spinnakers shade
rotted buildings, glistening condos.

The city muscled and bullied skyward.
The river, our *sheanachi* and *griot*, keeper of myth,
tells the other story: who lost.

This river tale is mine, is Chicago's, a history
as unsung as any in the flashpan of America's
rise from prairie and stream to a city
torn between the labor of slaves and immigrants
and the blueprints of city barons.

Silence slips the tumult of progress,
this wordless language of rivers
ever moving through dappled light.

ACKNOWLEDGMENTS

These poems previously appeared in the following journals
and anthologies:

America: "Praise"
Consequence: "Cloud of Witnesses"
Crosswinds Poetry Journal: "Dark River, Light Falling"
Dos Gatos Anthology: Bearing the Mask: "They Named Me Wolf"
Great Lakes Review: "In Spite of Debris, Offal, Trash, Detritus" and "Carp at the Gates"
Malpais Review: "Boy Heroes of Mexico"
Naugatuck River Review: "A Line Breaking"
New Madrid: "*Ná Géill, Nunca Abdicación*" and "Union Stockyards"
Poets Speak Anthology: Survival: "Chief Shabbona Speaks"
Poets Speak Anthology: Walls: "Magicians"
Portside Literary: "A Line Breaking"
Water~Stone: "SS Eastland Capsizes in the Chicago River"
Windhover: "Gamblers" and "Ruined"

The following are selective timelines.

Rio Grande

Praise, Preconquest: The Cochiti creation story says that the people who lived underground in the sacred place called Sipapu rose up through a hole in the earth to encounter the sun. God accompanied them through tribulations until they came to a land where the rain and sun would grow corn. In the Cochiti corn dance the people appeal to the deity Corn Mother for rain, for an abundance of crops and for fertility.

In the dance cornmeal is offered to Sun Father. Dancers chant, "Let the thunder be heard, O ye Ancients! Let the sky be covered with white blossom clouds, That the earth, O ye Ancients, Be covered with many colored flowers. That the seeds come up, That the stalks grow strong, That the people have corn."

The Chama and the Benedictines, 2016: The Monastery of Christ in the Desert, Abiquiu, New Mexico, was founded in 1964 by Fr. Aelred Wall, OSB. The monastery is seventy-five miles from Santa Fe. The monks follow a conservative Catholic theology. Their day begins with chanting of the psalms at 4:00 a.m., followed throughout the day by Lauds, Vespers, and Compline in the evening.

Passenger, 1528: Shipwrecked off the Florida coast, Álvar Núñez Cabeza de Vaca and Estevan the Moor were kept alive through the help of the Karankawa Indians and de Vaca's medical skills. Cabeza de Vaca returned to Spain in 1537 to report the deplorable violence Indians were suffering at the hands of the Spanish.

Meinrad's Call, 1966: Meinrad Craighead, American artist and mystic, painted and lectured in Spain and France in her twenties. Her stunning paintings are both dark and ecstatic. At thirty years old, she felt called to enter a monastery at Stanbrook Abbey in England. She remained there for fourteen years until, needing deeper solitude, she was called to the desert and the Rio Grande in 1980. She has remained as a hermit painter near the great river in Albuquerque, New Mexico.

Dream of the One-Footed, 1598: Soon after conquistador Juan de Oñate's expedition crossed the Rio Grande near El Paso, he proclaimed the land to be a province of Spain. In 1599 he waged war against Acoma Pueblos, leaving eight hundred villagers dead. In 1998, the four hundredth anniversary of his arrival, Acomas opposed to celebrating his life sawed off the right foot of a statue of Oñate.

Dark River, Light Falling, 1550: Bishop Bartolomé de las Casas is considered a primary initial defender of human rights. He defended the indigenous people by publicly indicting Spaniards who supported the *encomienda* system, which awarded land and native peoples as slaves to conquerors. He testified that *encomenderos* were guilty of a mortal sin and detailed their cruelty toward the native peoples.

God's Map: A Sonnet Crown, 2015: Stephen Manning was one of the first immigration lawyers from the American Immigration Lawyers Association (AILA) to go to Artesia Family Detention Center on the New Mexico–Mexican border to represent mothers and children who were being deported back to Central America where they feared both the police and the gangs. In Texas I met with mothers at a similar facility, the Karnes Family Detention Center, two weeks after seventy-seven women called a hunger strike to protest the conditions at the facility. The mothers were told by guards that because they were not caring for their children properly, the children could be taken by child welfare services if they kept up the fast.

2012–2016: If fleeing immigrants survive the 1,500-mile trip from their country through Mexico to the southern Texas border near Falfurrias and Del Rio, they may die of dehydration in Brooks County or drown in the Rio Grande. US Deputy Sergeant Benny Martinez's office daily receives emergency calls from migrants near collapse stranded somewhere in the 943 square miles of Brooks County, Texas. Martinez believes that the 129 deaths in the blistering fields of Brooks County in 2012 alone remains largely a preventable tragedy.

Gamblers, 2016: Fusion reported in *The Huffington Post* that 80 percent of women and girls are raped on their flight to the United States. Almost 40 percent of unaccompanied minors are girls. Sexual violence in Central America has risen at an alarming rate, as has the daily level of violence people face. In 2014, Immigration Customs Enforcement (ICE) apprehended 63,721 unaccompanied Central American children fleeing for their lives. Two-thirds of these children had no legal representation, without which many were deported. At the US southern border, those claiming critical fear of returning to their homelands increased from 5,369 in 2009 to 36,174 in 2013. By 2019, hundreds of unaccompanied minors were held in tent cities in Texas. Two children in custody died in December 2018—seven-year-old Jakelin Rosemary Cael Maquin died from cardiac arrest as a result of dehydration, and Felipe Gomez Alonzo died of flu on Christmas Eve. In 2019, Homeland Security had lost the placement of 1,475 children and were holding approximately 14,000 children in custody.

Lament, 2016: In May I met with mothers and kids on the night of their release from the Karnes Family Detention Center and was shocked to discover that the price of their expedited release was that they had to wear ankle braces and electronically report to ICE their whereabouts every few hours. They'll wear the anklets for months or years before their political asylum case is called. And these are the "lucky" ones who were not deported.

The Angel of Tenosique, 2016: Fleeing mothers name the devils on their journey through Mexico: the Zeta gang, police who demand bribes, border agents, and rapists. They also describe not simply kindness (such as "the angel of Tenosique") but Mexicans who risked their lives to protect or hide them.

Last Blessing, 2016: In El Salvador, gangs M18 and M13 function as extortionist enforcers who demand rent from both urban workers and *campesinos*. If a mother or father can no longer pay the *renta*, the gangs beat, kill, or force their adolescent son into the gang. Girls are made to sexually serve gang members. Mothers send their boys on the dangerous road north out of desperation. When Andrea (not her real name) fled after a gang murdered her two Guatemalan sons, she was denied entrance at the

US border three times. Only through legal assistance by the KINO Border Initiative was she sent to Eloy Detention Center where she awaits a court hearing.

Ná Géill, Nunca Abdicación, 1846–1847: The San Patricio Brigade was composed mostly of Irish immigrants but also some German, Italian, Polish, Scotch, and Spanish immigrants, as well as former slaves. Most were Catholics shocked by the killing of Mexican priests. US General Winfield Scott issued the order for the hanging of thirty San Patricios.

Boy Heroes of Mexico, 1846–1847: When Antonio Lopez de Santa Anna, the president of Mexico, rejected the American annexation of Texas, President James Polk declared war. In 1847, US forces advanced on the Castle of Chapultepec, a military school for boys aged thirteen to nineteen. Unlike the story Mexican children know, Juan Escutia was not a student at Chapultepec but a soldier from the Battalion of San Blas. He was killed in battle. The enduring truth, however, is that six cadets died defending Mexico.

Vows, 2016: Sister Norma Pimentel and a team of volunteers from Brownsville, Texas, have developed a program at Sacred Heart Church that sends buses to the border to pick up families and unaccompanied youth. When they arrive at the Sacred Heart auditorium and its makeshift tents, a welcome committee begins clapping. All because a nun from Catholic Charities was called one night and told there were hungry families sleeping on the floor of a bus station. In 2015 and 2016, the church served two hundred people a day. In 2014, when the surge began, volunteers were feeding and housing four hundred a day.

Tony and the Rio Grande, 1938–2015: Tony Mares was a poet, historian, essayist, and fiction writer. He was the gentlest of men and one who loved language, beauty, and nature, but not more than he loved justice for the poor and dispossessed. As a child he loved to play and swim along the Rio Grande. His children too walked the river's banks, accompanied by a father who taught them to "*listen to the river, breathe the land*."

Chicago River

The Leap, 1995: The day my mother died in our arms.

Magicians, 1836: Construction of the Illinois and Michigan Canal began on the Chicago River in 1836. Completed in 1848, it connected the Great Lakes to the Mississippi and the Gulf of Mexico. The canal workers were Irish immigrants and former slaves.

Lambs of God, 1854: St. James churchyard, which sits on a bluff above the Calumet Sag, is deserted. Its small adjacent cemetery has stone markers listed with the names of Irish canal diggers who attended St. James church.

Fouled, 1885: Because the Chicago River emptied into Lake Michigan, which was the people's source of drinking water, many Chicagoans were sickened; some died from typhoid.

Jacques Marquette's Canticle, 1673–1675: Marquette, a French Jesuit missionary, joined Louis Joliet to canoe to the northern part of the Mississippi. On return he stayed alone in a cabin on a Chicago portage for the winter. In spring, ill with dysentery, he left his portage cabin for the Grand Village of the Illinois tribe at Starved Rock, where he was welcomed by thousands. After Easter mass, Indian guides accompanied him back home to Michigan. He died just miles from St. Ignace.

Jean Baptiste Point du Sable's Patience, 1784: Jean Baptiste Point du Sable, a French-educated Haitian, was Chicago's first settler. He was a pioneer and trader who knew six languages and was an honorary member of the Potawatomi tribe. Du Sable was a successful farmer, trapper, and cattle owner whose homestead and trading post stood on what is now the location of the Tribune building.

Chief Shabbona's Vision, 1832: Shabbona of the Potawatomi tribe fought alongside Tecumseh as a young man, but he saw the futility of resisting white encroachment. When Sauk warrior Black Hawk sought his support for an uprising, he refused, saying, "The army of pale faces you will have to encounter will be as numerous as the leaves on those trees."

What do we know of the laws and customs of white people?, 1832: Black Hawk insisted that he never understood the treaty he signed that forced the tribe across the Mississippi to Iowa. With five hundred warriors and a thousand women and children, the Sauk leader crossed back to their Illinois lands. As a result of their defiance, two-thirds of the tribe died in battle or from starvation and illness.

Union Stockyards, 1865: By the 1900s, over 80 percent of the nation's beef was produced in the Yards. The Yards extracted one-half-million gallons of water a day and dumped or drained so much offal and waste into the south fork of the Chicago River that it produced gases resulting from the decomposition. To this day the river bubbles near the Yards.

I, Lucy Parsons, Am Still A Rebel, 1886: On May 1, eighty thousand workers walked off the job and marched down Michigan Avenue demanding an eight-hour workday. Leading the strike were Albert Parsons and his wife Lucy Parsons. Within days Chicago Mayor Harrison attended a worker's rally at Haymarket Square. He told Chief Bonfield that the crowd was nonviolent. Bonfield was nicknamed "Black Jack" because his police used billy clubs against striking workers at the McCormick plant. After the mayor and the Parsons left, Chief Bonfield ordered police to surround the rally. Someone threw dynamite, killing officers and protestors—seven in all. Eight labor and anarchist leaders were found guilty in spite of the testimony of witnesses that they were innocent. In 1887, four of the leaders, including Albert Parsons, were hung. During the hanging, Lucy and the children were kept in a police cell.

Mother Jones, Elizabeth Gurley Flynn, Big Bill Haywood, Lucy Parsons, and Eugene Debs founded the Industrial Workers of the World (the Wobblies). Lucy Parsons became the editor of their newspaper, *The Liberator*. She died penniless in a fire at age eighty-nine. Even in death she was a threat: the police confiscated all of her books and papers.

White City, 1893: The World's Columbian Exposition opened to international enthusiasm. Twenty-seven million people from all over the world came to the White City. The exposition covered six hundred acres, with close to two hundred neoclassical buildings, a promenade, canals, and lagoons.

SS Eastland *Capsizes in the Chicago River*, 1915: The *SS Eastland* was transporting Western Electric workers to a picnic in Michigan City, Indiana—an eagerly anticipated company free day for many who could not afford holidays. The steamer was swift but unbalanced. It crashed rapidly to one side, trapping some and flinging others into the river. Eight hundred people drowned in twenty feet of water.

A Line Breaking: 1919 Riots, 1919: Throughout 1918 there had been eleven fire bombings of African American buildings in the Black Belt of the United States. Black soldiers returning from World War I entered a postwar America about to explode. National strikes broke out, and police Red Squads were formed to deal with the socialist threat. In Chicago, a fourteen-year-old black boy drowned after being struck by a rock thrown by a white man, and a race war began. Chicago police arrested a black man instead of the culprit. The police turned a blind eye to violent retribution from white athletic clubs (gangs). Populist mayor Big Bill Thompson refused federal troops. Of the twenty-five racial wars that occurred nationally in the Red Summer of 1919, Chicago's was the bloodiest, lasting eight days.

Baptism, 1958: I left studying philosophy at Loyola University in my senior year in order to become an Adrian Dominican nun. My last teaching mission was at St. Theresa's, an African American school in what became a central riot area after Martin Luther King was killed. Forbidden to march or organize during the 1960s, I left the order after eight years.

Blood Red, 1984: Members of the Chicago Religious Task Force on Central America chose the anniversary of Archbishop Oscar Romero's martyrdom to dye the Chicago River red. Priests, ministers, rabbis, and nuns who'd been missionaries in Latin America were continually arrested during the 1980s for participating in protests against President Reagan's funneling $1.2 million a day for twelve years to the Salvadoran military responsible for the deaths of eighty thousand, mostly civilians.

Carp at the Gates, 2017: The city has a provisional goal to clean the Chicago River for swimming and fishing and to rid the river of invasive Asian carp. This may take years.